i was loosing you :
who we once were and who we have become
i can feel you slowly drifting away from me as if
you have never truly held on
its tiring watching you become someone that i no
longer recognize
its a hard concept in becoming so familiar with
someone
just to one day only remember them in idle things
such as pictures and faint memories
you are all that i once was
all that i held onto
now i fear you are the worst version
of yourself

aliza grace

meeting you was like listening to a song
for the very first time
knowing that no matter what i do
i will never get it out of my head
knowing that ill someday tell my kids about it
that it will forever be my favorite

you wont
find me
at the bottom
of a bottle

you will
find me
at home
waiting on you
to come
back
to me

-*realizing what you let go*

aliza grace

you never called to say sorry
you called to ask for your things back
the things that have set in a box in the dark room of
my house
the room i never go in anymore because it reminds
me of you

you never called to say sorry
you called to make small talk
because if you
cant get me
off your mind
why should i
be able to
get you off mine

aliza grace

whenever say i feel your pain
i dont mean the same boat
its the same ocean

aliza grace

the photographs we took never changed
but the guy in them did

aliza grace

you hugged me so tight
that i left with your scent on my shirt
and that was the last thing
you ever gave to me

aliza grace

sometimes late at night
our memories sneak out of my eyes
and roll down my cheek

1:00 am
you can drink all the alcohol you want
but you still wont forget the sound of her laugh

aliza grace

i cant remember what it was like before we met

maybe because i always imagined the idea of love

and as soon as you took a step in my life you fit
what i thought was the standard

aliza grace

its nights like these
were i wish i could
feel how much
i mean to you

aliza grace

in a room full of people
its still your face i search for
even though its been months

aliza grace

maybe in ten years our paths will cross again
we can meet over coffee
i will tell you how desperately in love
i was with you
and we can laugh about how
we broke each others hearts

aliza grace

if only you knew
how much tears ive cried
because of you

aliza grace

i wish i could be dainty for you
so that when you hear words like
divine and *angelic*
you think of me
i wish i could offer my heart to you
with the feminine finesse i know you crave
so that when you have it in your hands
there is no urge to let go
i wish i could be a sense of hope for you
so that your memories of me are attached
to all things beautiful
like sunshine and daisies
and fate
i wish i could give everything to you
but i know even that is not enough

aliza grace

sometimes i view myself
the way i think you would
and im conflicted between
thinking that your vision
is spiked with awe and wanting
the valleys of my collarbones
the curve of my nose
droopy eyes and soft chin
enticing you
the way you entice me
but i cant help but consider
the realistic scenario
you spotting the lifeless gaze
between the lashes you call home
disenchanted by the way
my body does not respond
because it has been wronged before
the truth is though
you probably dont view me at all
and thats what hurts the most

aliza grace

i want to be a girl
in the sense other girls are
they smell like summer
and always have the right
right words to say
poised and velvety
secure in their grace

their smiles are
innocent yet coy
and their body
compels instead of repels

even their tears
are enviable
delicately streaking
their soft pink cheeks
prom problems i wish to have

meanwhile ugly sobs
rock my broad shoulders
and harsh face
as i reconstruct
who i am
outside and inside
    just to have an ounce of their femininity

aliza grace

our love was timeless
but time ran out

aliza grace

i told you i loved you
but i was lying

aliza grace

in love with only a memory
loving you was a burden and a curse

aliza grace

i miss the old me
i miss the me i was with you

aliza grace

meeting you was such an important lesson
so was loosing you

aliza grace

"but baby, your just the ghost of someone i thought i knew."

aliza grace

something felt familiar in your face

aliza grace

i dont romanticize love anymore
what i mean by that is you used to be
the first thing i would think about when
i woke up and the last thing i would think
just before i went to bed

but now i dont think of you
or anyone for that matter
perhaps you have changed me
or perhaps i have just grown up

aliza grace

in love with a memory

aliza grace

dont you think if you
really love something
a little bit of it will
always linger

aliza grace

if what we have isnt natural
then why is loving you
the easiest thing ive ever had to do
i suppose you are my forbidden fruit
together we can make it out of the garden
into a world that holds so much hatred
we will have to love twice as hard
to make up for their sins
to never be separated from you

aliza grace

i close my eyes
and im haunted with
what could have been
and who could have been

there were so many things
i could have done differently
and its all i think of
to the point where i ignore
everything else
around me

scared to make the same mistakes

aliza grace

you are a woman who has had
everything she needs within her self
since she was born into this world

aliza grace

i sleep
instead of crying
i quit
without even trying
my days are all the same
and my poetry is lame
you seem to be the only thing
to make me smile

aliza grace

if you look close enough
in the night sky
its still the same moon
i would have gotten you

aliza grace

you always loved the stars
infact i grew to love them too
its funny how they shined brighter

now that youve joined them

aliza grace

we have run out of pages
my love
our story is over

aliza grace

she set fire to her entire world but never let a single flame touch him

aliza grace

they broke each other with the purest intentions
they didnt have a clue what love meant
they did their best until
they couldnt anymore

aliza grace

everybody always told her
to stay away from the edge
because she could fall
what they didnt realize
was that was exactly
what she wanted

aliza grace

everything you said to me i fell in love with
but now it scares me
how different those word sound now

aliza grace

you were my dream come true
but i was never yours
im trying my best to let go of you
its hardest to let go of
what could have been

aliza grace

you will keep going for him
because even after he ended his time
you still have to continue yours
do it for him

aliza grace

til death tears us apart
they said

but i disagree
not even death can tear
away my body from yours
because its my soul thats attached

aliza grace

as her sadness consumed her
she came to realise she had not lost herself
but had lost the person
she used to be

now we are just strangers who show up
but dont matter enough to each other
to be friends

we have too much history to be strangers

aliza grace

you know what the saddest part is

the thing that hurts the most

everything around me reminds me of him

you wanna know what the good part is

thats all i have left of him

aliza grace

she had so much love to give
so she could feel the deepest pains
see the widest smiles
in the end
it was her compassion that killed her

aliza grace

maturing is realizing
nothing lasts forever

aliza grace

i must
have a crazy
imagination if
i still think
youll come back

aliza grace

getting over him is possible
it will take time
but it will happen
slowly but surely it will happen
youll get the urge to go out again
youll meet new people
moving on will taste sweet
seeing yourself find happiness
all over again
building back up the confidence
he destroyed

soul candy

aliza grace

you never seen me
for who i was
you only seen what you wanted

aliza grace

its hard i know
life is hard
and if your
giving it all
you can
thats enough
and im proud

aliza grace

you torture yourself stalking her instagram
you know what your doing
you just cant stop

comparing yourself

aliza grace

social media is killing us all
and we are setting idle
watching it happen

aliza grace

letting go
can make you feel
every emotion

more emotions
then you thought
you had

but i promise
youll feel better

it just takes time

aliza grace

who is it
the person
who made you
scared to love again

aliza grace

do you ever think about me too

aliza grace

being alone
and feeling lonely
they are two different things

aliza grace

i wish i could have frozen time
all of those times spent in your arms

aliza grace

i must hate myself
to want to be with you still
even though i know you dont
love me knowing you never cared

aliza grace

im not sad
just disappointed

aliza grace

its okay
im fine

3:00 am
im awake listening
to your favorite song

replaying memories
in my head

maybe ill see you
in my dreams

aliza grace

love is really
bittersweet

aliza grace

your
killing me
with the silence

aliza grace

tell me we will be okay
even if we arent

aliza grace

why do you leave
only to return
when i convince myself
im over you

aliza grace

i hope you
find it one day
whatever it is

aliza grace

i
will
never
forget
how
you
made
me
feel

aliza grace

youve been working
on yourself
and it shows

aliza grace

we are now in
each others lifes
for a reason
thank you
for showing up

aliza grace

start now
start where you are
start with fear
start with passion
start with failing and messing up
youve got to start somewhere

soul candy

aliza grace

there is love
in holding on
there is love is
letting go

aliza grace

we are all
products of our past

aliza grace

if you are thinking
of letting me go
then i think
its time
you do that

aliza grace

you havent met
who you will ever
love yet

soul candy

aliza grace

you were my
first love

aliza grace

pain
is never
permanent

aliza grace

why does it
still hurt

*because it really
meant something*

aliza grace

people start healing
the moment
they feel heard

aliza grace

something about you
is like an addiction

aliza grace

even if we never speak to one another

please

remember that im forever changed by you

and what you meant to me

aliza grace

life is short
go after
whatever it is
you love

aliza grace

if we dont tell people
how we feel
how will they know

aliza grace

it was a privilege to love you
and
it was a privilege to let you go

aliza grace

dont hold me back
let me go

let me go with grace

aliza grace

find what youd die for
and live for it

aliza grace

stop opening doors back up
for toxic people you shut out
and calling it closure

aliza grace

never let people destroy your peace
because they are at war with themselves

aliza grace

im sorry
they made
you feel
like your
hard to
love

no one
is hard
to
love

aliza grace

you change people
your name makes me smile
your work moves people
your name makes my heart beat a little faster

its you

we were something
werent we

dont you think so

aliza grace

someone
out here
will be so
gentle
and
soft
with
your heart

aliza grace

loving you came
so natural to me

aliza grace

if your constantly
trying to prove
your worth
to someone else you
have already
forgotten your value

aliza grace

may we all heal
from things
we dont speak
about

aliza grace

the only way to
trust again
is by
trusting again

aliza grace

hurting them back
will not heal your pain

aliza grace

if your heart
tells you
something
does not
feel right
dont ignore
it

aliza grace

first love
doesnt mean
best love

aliza grace

forgive yourself
for accepting
less than you deserve

and then never do it again

aliza grace

sometimes people
are on journeys
that we are
not a part of

aliza grace

its just a person
they shouldnt make
you so nervous

aliza grace

love will find you
when you stop looking

aliza grace

you still have so many years
to meet so many people

aliza grace

to everything
ive lost:

thank you
for setting me
free

aliza grace

i hope you know how much
meeting you has changed my life

aliza grace

all endings
are also
beginnings

aliza grace

being with someone
should heal your soul
more than hurt it

soul candy

aliza grace

i hope one day you realize that you deserve
the world and should
stop settling for the bare minimum

aliza grace

normalize
admitting
you care

aliza grace

someday you will
look back on all
the progress you made
and be so glad you
did not give up

aliza grace

healthy love
exists
and its worth
being patient for

aliza grace

you are not
unloveable
because people
have treated you
poorly

aliza grace

dont ruin a good today
by thinking about
a bad yesterday

aliza grace

go and laugh in all the same places
youve cried
change the narrative

aliza grace

love did not hurt you
someone who does not know
how to love you hurt you
never confuse the two

aliza grace

you deserve a love that stays even when
it rains
especially when
it rains

aliza grace

you deserve love
that is deeper than the
ocean

dont settle
for a
stream

aliza grace

stop folding yourself
into halve when
the whole of you
is a masterpiece

<u>good news:</u>
you *will* over it
just like you got over
that other thing

aliza grace

being alone is always better
than being with someone
who does not value who
you really are

aliza grace

you have so many parts of
yourself to meet still

aliza grace

you deserve the empathy
you give others

aliza grace

hurts me 217 times

*maybe i should give them a
second chance*

aliza grace

its okay to be sad
after making the
right decision

aliza grace

do you really
want someone
you have to beg
to stay

aliza grace

be kind

everyone is still healing

from things left

unsaid

aliza grace

people need more love than they show

aliza grace

be the reason
someone
feels
seen
heard
and
supported

aliza grace

remember
sometimes
the way
you think
about a
person
is not
the way
they actually
are

aliza grace

your idea of me
is not my
responsibility
to live up to

aliza grace

dont feel
guilty
doing whats
best for you

Made in the USA
Monee, IL
04 January 2023